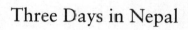

Three Days in Nepal

Three Days in Nepal

JeanDavid Blanc

Translated by Chris Murray

Collins

Three Days in Nepal
Copyright © 2013 by JeanDavid Blanc
All rights reserved.

Published by Collins, an imprint of HarperCollins Publishers Ltd

First Canadian edition

HarperCollins books may be purchased for educational, business, or sales promotional use through our Special Markets Department.

HarperCollins Publishers Ltd
2 Bloor Street East, 20th Floor
Toronto, Ontario, Canada
M4W 1A8

www.harpercollins.ca

ISBN 978-1-44342-402-8

Printed and bound in the United States
RRD 9 8 7 6 5 4 3 2 1

This is a true story.

*I have tried to remember everything exactly as it happened, to
capture my feelings and the thoughts that crossed my mind
over the course of those three days.*

*The dialogues are reconstructed as faithfully as possible,
and the text messages are copied and pasted from
those still stored in my phone.*

Foreword

Nothing compares with the feeling of flight. I don't mean sitting in an airplane, but flying on your own, by your own power—feeling flight to your very core, piloting with your muscles and reflexes, your body airborne like a bird.

When I was about ten years old, I had a dream. All I had to do was to push with my legs, hold out my arms, and I would take off like Superman. I would soar over houses, skim over fields and roads and circle through the air like a bird. When I woke up, I felt like I had really flown.

As soon as I could afford to, I took flying lessons. I joined a flying club. I was taught the theory of piloting and how to take off in little airplanes. But I never redis-covered the feeling of my childhood dream. Planes are

1

practical for getting from point A to point B, from one airport to another, but apart from takeoff and landing, you don't really feel like you're flying.

Much later, I discovered powered paragliding. It involves wearing a strange machine with a motor and a propeller strapped to your back that turns your body into a plane. A giant wing that, when given some speed, lifts you into the air. An entire powered paraglider, or PPG, can be folded up into two bags that fit in the trunk of a car or can be checked as luggage.

The PPG is like a costume that turns you into a flying animal. You can fly low like a dragonfly or as high as an eagle, as slowly as a butterfly or as swiftly as a falcon. The very best pilots can touch down on a moving bus or land on an egg in the middle of a field.

Powered paragliding is not a very popular sport. It requires dedication, not to mention time and patience. You have to learn to watch the weather and read the clouds, know your motor inside and out, manipulate the wing and monitor the air that keeps it afloat. Only once you've mastered these skills does the sport yield its reward: the joy of flying wherever, whenever and however you want. The PPG is the most reliable aircraft in the world—as long as you remain humble.

Powered paragliding is also a great way to meet people from different walks of life—it attracts people who are outgoing and adventurous and often both loners and

team players at the same time. It's a mindset: the act of
flying is in itself an individual act, but most people fly in
groups. I've met a number of lone wolves, of course, but
most pilots would rather fly in the company of others,
like a flock of birds.

That's how I came to meet François, Efi, Adam and
Laurent, pilots who have become my friends and with
whom I often go on powered paragliding trips. A powered paragliding trip involves setting off to discover a
new country with our machines in tow. Once we arrive,
we meet other pilots, both local and foreign. The locals
(who often organize the tours) serve as guides, showing
us their country from the air. We usually go on two to
three flights per day, very early in the morning or in the
late afternoon and early evening, so that there is as little
wind as possible.

I think it was Efi who first spoke to me about a January
tour being organized in Nepal. When I told François
about it, we decided to go together.

The tour had been arranged by a couple of Russian
expats, flying enthusiasts who had lived in Pokhara for a
long time. Pokhara is a town situated at the foot of the
Himalayas and is a world-renowned base camp for trekkers and hippies alike. Natasha, her husband and their son,
Stephan, had started a flying club there, giving tourists an

opportunity to discover the exceptional Himalayan beauty of Mount Everest and Annapurna from the air.

Winter was the best time of year for flying, thanks to low winds and the lift provided by cold air.

The opportunity to discover Nepal in such ideal conditions was a dream come true.

Prologue

A *tailwind is pushing me toward my destination. The sun is in front of me, radiant. I have music in my ears, full blast. I often fly listening to soundtracks from films. Mainly action movies. In flight, this music takes on a whole other dimension. There is a layer of clouds beneath me. The other pilots have stayed below it and are fighting a crosswind, but I'm moving fast. This is the first time that I've flown above the clouds, like a commercial jet. The clouds gradually thicken below me until I can't see the ground at all. I shouldn't have let this happen: If my motor gives out, I won't be able to locate a place to land. I am using my GPS to navigate.*

It had been eight days already since a group of pilots from all around the world had come together to take part in this power paragliding trip. The "Russian team," as we called them, was made up of six people: a couple from Siberia (although the wife didn't fly; she was just along for the ride) and four other pilots, including Viktor, a European champion. Most of the time, they kept to themselves. They were all nice enough, but had already created their own little group, which spoke poor English. And our Russian was non-existent. Laurent, a three-time PPG world champion, had come from Canada. There were two pilots from Belgium, one especially funny guy from Brazil, Efi and Adam from Israel, and François and me from France. We had just spent the week flying over Nepal from one region to another, taking to the sky several times a day. The organizers of the Nepal PPG Trek had done an excellent job. Each flight was different from the one before and allowed us to discover the country from a new perspective.

I had lost visual contact with François, but the Brazilian pilot had followed me. I could see the Russian team, who had taken off ahead of me, in the distance. Thanks to the tailwind, I was quickly catching up to them. Having reached the target destination on my GPS, I began my descent through the clouds. I couldn't see anything, but I knew I was above our point of arrival. To spice things up a bit, I cut off the motor. The sail, freed from the motor's propulsion, transformed into a paraglider. I turned off the music.

Descending through the clouds in near silence, the

wind whistling through the lines of my sail, felt incredible. Just a few hundred metres below, part of the team was already on the ground. I flew toward them and touched down like a feather. What a thrill! My first instrument flight!

That evening we arrived in Pokhara, where we planned to spend the last two days of the trip. A PPG tournament involving various flying contests had been organized for the following day: games like catching a ball with your feet and throwing it into a ring of hay bales or slaloming figure eights around inflatable pylons. Games for birds, in a way.

Pokhara is a lively place at night, though we rarely took advantage of it. To fly early in the morning, we usually went to bed at a reasonable time. That night, however, we wanted to enjoy the town's great ambience. The crowd was a mix of trekkers leaving on or coming back from expeditions, free-spirited hippies and Western meditation enthusiasts. One bar had live music, and some of us who were musicians found ourselves joining in with the band, playing jazz, blues and rock and roll. The wife of the Siberian pilot, seemingly shy, turned out to be a real rock star on stage, playing the drums with an energy you'd never have suspected her capable of.

The next day would be our last day of flying before everyone returned home on Saturday. Stephan and his parents had planned a flight worthy of the occasion, the ultimate Pokhara experience: We would soar over the foothills of the Himalayas toward Annapurna.

It was to be the high point of our stay.

I

The Flight

I entered the coordinates into my GPS. Our goal was Korchon, about 16 kilometres further north, at over 3,000 metres, about 2,500 metres higher than Pokhara itself. François took off first, and after an initial failed attempt, I followed. It was eleven in the morning.

François gained altitude quickly and soon cleared the first crest of the mountain, about 1,000 metres above our takeoff point. I'm usually wary of flying over mountains— the air can seem completely calm on one side, only to give way to sudden turbulence and dangerous downdrafts on the other. I flew over the first crest with a wide margin of safety. François and I stayed in radio contact but soon lost sight of each other. A light mist began to form. From the other side of the mountain, I could see a cloud bank to the north. It seemed like nothing to worry about, but some of the other pilots decided to head home. This wasn't surprising; at high altitude you need the right protection against the cold and a reasonably powerful motor to keep climbing.

At about 2,500 metres, François radioed to say that he was too cold and had decided to give up. A few minutes later his motor died anyway, which sometimes happens. A breakdown doesn't mean you fall—the wing continues gliding—but you have to be on the lookout for a place to land in the event of an emergency. After some difficult manoeuvres back around the mountain, avoiding power lines, houses and cliffs, François landed near a road without incident.

Things were still going well for me. It's a surprisingly comfortable feeling to be high in the air and far away from it all, even in the cold of winter in the Himalayas. The motor was humming away, and I was dressed warmly enough to keep going. The landscape was breathtaking. In the distance ahead I could make out the vastness of the Himalayas. A tiny white temple sat isolated in the valley below. Behind me, in the middle of the fields, lay our takeoff point.

As I made headway, visibility started to worsen. In a matter of moments I couldn't see anything. The mist had become so thick that I felt like I was wrapped in cotton. There was no turning back now—it would have been impossible to see any obstacles below. My only option was to keep climbing and try to get above the thick layer of clouds, as I had done the day before. Being in the middle of what seems like pea soup is very strange—you know you're hanging in mid-air, but you can't see a thing. I felt a vague dizziness that was almost pleasant. With my eyes pinned to the GPS, I could see that I was still climbing. I knew I'd eventually get above the clouds. Besides, what was the risk? It wasn't as if I was going to run into anything, and there wasn't any other air traffic. I just hoped I had enough fuel to get back safely.

Like a diver going deeper and deeper underwater, I began to feel an exhilaration I'd never known before. Safely wrapped in my white cotton, I navigated somewhat drunkenly, deep into the tummy of an endless cloud.

The air got colder. I couldn't see more than a metre in any direction, and everything was the same shade of white. It's disorienting, dizzying, to look around and find yourself suspended in the fog. There was no reason to feel this way—I was like a pendulum, the laws of gravity don't change with altitude. I was obviously still hanging from my sail, upright, with the earth below, but I found it was better not to look up because it gave me the impression that I was turning upside-down. I'd rather keep my eyes on the GPS, which showed that I wasn't far from my destination—only a kilometre or two away as the crow flies, and 300 metres higher up the mountain. At that point, I couldn't see anything. The cloud got so thick that I could barely see my own knees.

A new wave of dizziness took over as I suddenly saw the ground coming straight at me, a metre or so away, like a mirage. Time stood still. I tried to figure out what was happening. The ground couldn't be in front of me, I reasoned. Was I hallucinating, delirious, or was it vertigo? The ground was getting closer, but too slowly for it to feel like a fall, and I glanced up to see my sail still stable, flying strong above me. As long as it was still flying, then that meant I was still suspended vertically below it. It was uncanny, as if everything was unfolding in slow motion, giving me the time to formulate what was happening. Then, suddenly, everything made sense: If that wasn't the ground, it had to be the mountains. I was about to slam into a rock face. I braked as hard as I could to turn the sail around, but it was too late. I crashed into the side of the mountain.

My attempt to turn did serve some purpose, however. As I hit the rock wall, the cage, propeller and motor took the brunt of the impact, sparing me. Slowly, as if in a time warp, I saw and felt everything. Nothing was sudden or violent. The blow was distinct but gentle, and as I came to a stop, I found myself clinging to a bush.

Everything was calm. The noise of the motor and the wind rushing past me had stopped. I was bathed in silence.

The sail settled on the branches of the bush, the lines whispering past my face as they fell. I was unhurt except for a small graze on my nose. To think—I had crashed into the side of a mountain and come out with just a scrape!

I quickly realized that even if I hadn't hurt myself in the crash, I could now just as easily fall like a stone to the earth below. After all, I had ascended 3,000 metres. There was nothing below me but a sheer drop. I gripped my branches a little tighter and hoped they would hold.

I took a timid glance downwards, but the fog was too dense to make anything out. I was still enveloped in a cloud of white cotton, a blind man perched on a shrub, hanging over the abyss.

II

Perched on a Bush

The fog was thickening. I tightened my grip, the motor still strapped to my back. The sail covered the top of the bush and the dangling lines tickled my nose. I could only hear a light breeze and the sound of my own breathing, which was amplified in the foggy silence and by the headphones over my ears.

I took stock of my situation. So far, so good. I wasn't hurt. In fact, I didn't feel bad at all. I couldn't help imagining what I looked like from afar, a guy in a black and yellow jumpsuit, wearing headphones and a motor strapped to his back, clinging to a bush on the side of a mountain at 3,000 metres in the Himalayas. Legs tucked in, knees tight, my arms hugging the branches, like Wile E. Coyote from Road Runner or George of the Jungle hanging on for dear life . . . I smiled, though it was probably an adrenaline rush.

I realized how lucky I was. I could have ricocheted off a bare façade and dropped like a rock. But a bush had been there. I was in one piece, not particularly comfortable, but still alive. Oddly enough, instead of panic I felt a new state of elation.

The mist was so dense that I couldn't see further than my extended arms. Before doing anything else, I gauged my means of communication with the rest of the group. I grabbed my phone from my pocket and saw that, by some miracle, I had service. Then, I checked my GPS. I decided to communicate by text message rather than call for help; it would be a more reliable means of transmitting GPS coordinates—a string of numbers that would be difficult to understand if the connection was bad and the person on the other end spoke a different language. I texted three people at once: Stephan, who had organized the trip, François and Efi. That way, at least one of the three would read it.[1]

ME
Mayday! Crash on mountain N28
23 32.7 E83 56 27.0 alt 2959m

---

1 All of the text messages are transcriptions of the originals, including typos and spelling errors. Only the French has been translated, as necessary.

ME
No injuries but Can't move up
I'm on the side. Please confirm
you got my SOS. Please don't
call use SMS to communicate.
Or Radio 150.00

A few minutes went by before Stephan wrote back:

STEPHAN
OK. SAMBUDY ON THE WAY

ME
OK. Stuck at vertical dont know
how they will get to me

ME
Stephan, shall I try to go up?

STEPHAN
WHAT DO YOU MIN?

ME
I'm on side of mountain. No way to climb.

Then I decided to try addressing François directly.

ME
François, did you get my message?

EFI
DO NOT DO ANYTHING.
WAIT FOR INSTRAKTION

ME
Ok I won't move. What is the status?

EFI
WAIT AND KEEP YOURSELF WARM

ME
I'm ok. Wish i had cigarette

ME
Is François with you?

EFI
NO

At that same moment, I received a text from Valerie, a close friend back in France who was going through a difficult time. She's from Quebec and always talks to me in a sort of Franglais. Of course, she had no idea what had just happened to me. She just knew that I was crazy about flying and that I had gone on a PPG trip.

> VALERIE
> *Cant talk to anyone....its ter-*
> *rible....cant wait for u to be back*

> ME
> *Me too ;) Not for same reason*

> VALERIE
> *Lollll! Probably sur ton paramo-*
> *teur.... Tranquille.... by yourself...*
> *quel bonheur!*

> ME
> *If only you knew...*

> Valerie
> *Ok... but get back please*

> ME
> *I'm trying...*

Then, at the same moment:

> CECILIA
> *I think of you*

I had met Cecilia a few months earlier in Los Angeles. We hadn't had the chance to speak since then.

THOMAS
When do you get back????

ME
In theory, tomorrow...

The text messages were starting to add up; they weren't helping my rescue and were using up my already low battery. I thought it best not to bring up the details of my current situation. If the news were to reach my daughter or my parents, they'd be sick with worry. I decided not to say anything to anyone who couldn't directly contribute to my rescue, and certainly not to my friends and family back in Paris.

My radio still worked and was fully charged. Here, too, the signal was surprisingly strong and static-free. I would be able to talk to the ground team by radio. It would be reassuring to hear real voices. So I turned off my phone to save the battery.

ME TO GROUND TEAM
Shutting off phone only 20% bat.
Use radio 150.00 to contact

But I couldn't bring myself to turn off my phone without sending one last message. This one would be for my daughter. We were used to being in touch several times a day, mostly through text messages, especially on even-numbered days. For Rebecca and me, "even days"[2] were those when we would call each other "for sure." We systematically ended all of our texts with "Luv u." I couldn't be sure that I'd have service when I turned my phone back on, and anything could happen between now and then. What if I didn't get out of this as easily as I hoped? What if this was to be my last text? I had to message my daughter. But what could I tell her? I didn't want her to worry, but I didn't want to lie to her by pretending nothing was wrong.

I found myself faced with a question I had never thought I'd ask myself: What do you say in a text message that could be your last? I didn't have to think for very long—the answer was obvious.

ME TO REBECCA
I love you

This time, I spelled it out.
And I turned off my phone.

---

2   In French, even-numbered days are *jours pairs*, and *pair* is a play on *père* ("father").

III

Finding Refuge

I had to get out of this bush and onto solid ground. I couldn't see anything, and the steep drop was still below me. First, I had to get the PPG off my back without letting go of it or the bush. Then I needed to unhook the sail and sort out the lines that had gotten tangled in the branches. With some difficulty, I managed to ease out of the harness that kept the motor attached to my back and wedge the whole contraption against the rock. I was freed from my machine, but still hanging from the edge of the mountain.

I couldn't hold out in mid-air for long, with only the strength of my arms and my legs to rely on. I had to get into a more comfortable position, or at least a seated one, while I waited for help. I scanned my surroundings but still couldn't see beyond the branches of the bush and the nearest slabs of rock. From time to time the fog cleared slightly, revealing passing, ghostlike visions that vanished as quickly as they appeared. I could make out a completely vertical rock face to my right. Above me, a totally inaccessible wall of rocks; to my left, some stones and scrubby vegetation.

A tree suddenly emerged mirage-like from the mist. Its trunk seemed to grow horizontally from the rock wall before turning skyward. I told myself that if I could just make it to the tree, I could sit astride its trunk. But then it disappeared. I kept looking toward the place it had been, hoping to catch a second glimpse. The tree would have given me a place to wait in safety without worrying about a fall. When the mist parted again a few minutes later, I spotted a way to get to it by a series of hand- and foot-holds: rocks, branches, anything I could hold on to. The tree seemed to be about 20 metres away—which is a long way across a vertical rock face. I had no choice: I had to climb in that direction. I left my equipment behind and set out slowly. Not being able to see anything turned out to be a blessing. I would never have found the courage to move if I had been able to see the empty drop below me.

From stone to stone, root to root, I moved across the sheer surface like a mountaineer, holding on to anything

I could find. Limb after limb I crept forward, my nose against the face of the mountain. Then, a surprise—the tree grew out of the side, and just behind it was what appeared to be a small platform, a sort of balcony in mid-air. Not only could I sit down, I could even stretch out and walk a few paces. With a tent I could have even set up a little camp. I radioed my friends.

"Anyone listening?"

"Yes, this is Stephan. How are you, JeanDavid?"

"I'm fine. Listen, I found a place to stay safe. I'm sending you the coordinates by SMS. Not far from the other place, maybe 20 metres, but I'll send you the new coordinates anyway."

"OK. We try to send you choppers. On the way to the airport now. Don't worry, we'll get you out very soon!"

"OK, I'll wait. Keep me posted. Bye."

This would all be over in a few hours . . .

IV

Settling In

I still couldn't see much of my surroundings, but the fog was starting to dissipate. I had, at best, two or three square metres around me. A few sparse, frost-covered shrubs grew between the rocks. I wasn't protected from the elements, but at least I could sit down.

I waited. The ground was cold and hard, the air damp and icy. I was alone, in silence and whiteness. The mist billowed past peacefully as I wondered what to do next. I might need my sail or the rest of my equipment—but they had both stayed tangled in the bush. Should I go back and try to salvage what I could, risking a fall that I had just escaped, simply for a damaged motor? I hesitated. Alone, up there, sitting and doing nothing, time dragged on. I kept thinking about my precious equipment. I decided to head back as carefully as I could.

I set out on a first trip to the bush to retrieve the motor, all the while wondering what purpose it could possibly serve. I would have to come back across the quasi-vertical rock wall with my bare hands, holding a fifty-pound machine in one of them and risking a fall over the precipice. I went slowly, one handhold at a time. On the way back to the ledge, the weight of the motor threw me off balance. I stopped and tried to find my centre of gravity, my calm and concentration. I was very hot. I thought of the scene at the beginning of *Mission Impossible*, where Tom Cruise clings bare-handed to the side of a mountain and freezes in terror after narrowly avoiding a fall.

Getting the sail was another story. It took me nearly half an hour to free the lines, one by one, and the fabric. On several occasions, I almost fell when I reached out too far, trying to pull in a recalcitrant cable. When I finally got the sail on the ledge, I untangled it carefully and put it away in the bag that I always kept in my harness. I could stuff the sail away without folding it, and the bag looked like a big pouffe when it was full. I could sit or even lie on it comfortably. Looking at that bag always brought back a wave of memories—it was designed and made in Israel and had been given to me by Jimmy. Jimmy was one of my PPG friends and a terrific pilot, a man with a huge heart who had died tragically in a terrorist attack in Israel. He was so passionate about flying that he sometimes even looked like a bird. Thanks to him, my time stranded in the mountains was a little more bearable.

It had been almost four hours since my crash. I wasn't injured, had salvaged all of my equipment and had found a place to wait. I had avoided a fall that would have been fatal, or even worse, near-fatal. I was alive, high on adrenaline; I was even feeling good. When you escape the worst, everything else seems sweet.

I decided to take inventory. I had the motor (no longer really in working condition), the harness, the sail in its bag and a fanny pack. I remembered that, following a friend's advice, I had stored a survival blanket in my harness pocket. It would come in handy this time. I opened the pocket, but the survival blanket was gone; I must have taken it out to lighten the load of my luggage. Pity. I had a few rudimentary tools (a screwdriver, a set of Allen wrenches and some zip-ties) and some old hand warmers. In the fanny pack were my camera, my GPS, an iPod nano, a GoPro camera (in its box), copies of my ID and some money. I went through my pockets. Apart from my wallet and my iPhone, as luck would have it I found a fun-size candy bar—three little squares of chocolate. It was no bigger than my little finger, but better than nothing. I had hardly eaten any breakfast that morning, and this would be a source of sugar. I took care to save it for later, when I could ration it out if I needed to. For the time being I wasn't really hungry.

All this amounted to my survival equipment.

The radio crackled to life.

"JeanDavid, this is Viktor."

Viktor was one of the Russians. He had an elegant, athletic build and looked a little like Daniel Craig. My friends and I thought he had been in the FSB, the Russian special services that had replaced the KGB. Or at least that's what we imagined. He had, at the very least, been in the army and gone through some serious training.

"Yes, Viktor?"

"JeanDavid, you have to follow my instructions."

"What instructions?"

"First, you have to find yourself a safe place, protected from the wind and bad weather. I tell you: Now it's daytime, but it's gonna be night soon and you're gonna get cold."

He was right; I was already getting chilly. The fog was damp and heavy, and it was January at 3,000 metres in the Himalayas. I had been so glad not to have fallen to my death that I hadn't really grasped how cold it already was—pretty damn cold.

"Then you'll have to try to make yourself a camp, and if possible make a fire . . . We can't send choppers today because of bad weather. We sent a rescue team on the ground to find you, but they'll need at least twenty-four hours of walking to reach you. You'll have to prepare yourself for a long and lonely wait, my friend."

"OK, but hurry up, guys, because it's cold and kind of lonely here!"

"Well, you will spend the night there. You have to be prepared. You're not trained for that; it's gonna be hard. Both physically and psychologically. Use your wing to protect yourself."

Huh? I'm going to have to spend the night out here? Well, it wasn't like I really had a choice. How hard could it be? Admittedly I was alone in the mountains, but alive, and I had a safe place to wait, and they had my GPS coordinates—it would just be a night out under the stars. One way or another they would find me and get me out. I just had to wait. The mere fact that I had survived was enough to keep up my morale. I had my feet on solid ground, and I was unharmed. That was all that really mattered to me.

"Don't worry, I'm perfectly fine."

Viktor seemed to know what he was talking about. He had a firm and clear voice, a precise and reassuring way of expressing himself. He must have seen worse. Stephan, however, was more hesitant and wasn't quite sure what to do. Viktor had probably dealt with situations like this in the past; I could tell he had guided rescue missions before—or at least he gave the impression that he knew what he was doing. It was like in a movie where a stranded character has to radio for help.

"OK. Now you should shut down the radio to keep battery. We will keep our radio open all the time. Please contact us every hour, or at any time if emergency. We will update you with the situation."

"OK. Talk to you in an hour."

I turned off the radio.

V

Making a Fire

It was getting colder and colder. And I was going to have to spend the night out in the open. A fire would be nice. A fire keeps you company—its movement makes you feel like it's alive. It would also give me some light, and darkness was falling. Most of all, it would keep me warm, and tending it would keep me occupied and distracted. I could hunt for fuel to keep it alive, feed it little by little, adjust the wood to keep it going. I knew I had to make a fire, but I didn't have any way to start one. I had quit smoking a few months earlier and no longer carried a lighter or matches. Everything around me was covered in a layer of ice.

But night was coming, so I decided to try to look anyway, for anything that might burn. There were some dead branches on the tree and a few frozen bushes growing from the rocks. After a bit of searching and foraging, I managed to collect a little pile of wood. I had ventured out onto the tree to break off a few branches, but blinded by the fog, I avoided getting too close to the edge. I eventually found enough to feed a fire. I surrounded the wood with a circle of rocks, just like in an old Western.

I had seen people spin one piece of wood on another until it caught fire, so I gave it a shot. All of the wood was damp or frozen, though, and after a few attempts it was clear that the technique wasn't working well. I took a break and went over my inventory a second time, going through my pockets in the hope of finding a forgotten lighter. But there was nothing. Then my gaze fell on the PPG. If I could start the motor, I'd have the means of generating a spark. I could use it to start a fire one way or another. There might still be some gas in the tank. I took out the battery and examined it. There was about a quarter litre of gas left. How would I ever have finished my flight? I probably wouldn't have had enough fuel to reach my destination. Ironically, this accident might well have saved my life.

I detached the battery's electrical wires to create a short-circuit. There was no margin for error—if I managed to generate a single spark, it had to be the one to start the fire. I emptied part of the gas tank on the driest branches in my fire circle, then brought the battery closer and crossed the two wires. A spark jumped out in a blinding flash. I reeled back instinctively, but the gasoline instantly caught fire. I was ecstatic! I had done it! I had actually started a fire! Perched on a ledge, stranded high in the mountains, I had managed to reproduce the civilizing miracle that had made mankind. I had "made" fire, gone from darkness to light! I was quite proud of myself. Alone, lost, but happy.

I love log fires. I've always been able to "feel" fire, and I know it likes me too. When I was little, I spent hours tending our family fireplace, organizing the position of the logs, like building blocks. Leaving air below so the fire could breathe, giving it space when needed, making sure the logs were touching but not on top of one another. When a fire is happy, it shows. It puffs up its chest and blazes with majesty. When well-fed, a fire lightens, sings, dances, warms and smells good. But when it's upset, it becomes shy and hides, suffocates, sends smoke signals and then disappears. If you push the wood just a few centimetres, it comes back to life. Sometimes you just have to blow gently in the right place and give a coaxing whisper for it to come surging back. A fire is a generous, living thing.

I had a companion now, some light and warmth. I redoubled my efforts to find anything to keep it going. I tried to break off whatever dead wood I could find, gathering even the smallest twigs scattered on the ground—I kept this fuel in reserve, thawing it out next to the flames.

I felt I deserved a reward for my hard work, so I decided to immortalize my creation by taking a few pictures with my GoPro.

VI

Team Spirit

Night was falling. I felt increasingly isolated, stuck on my ledge perched high on the mountain. I turned on the radio.

"Hello? Anyone there?"

I waited a moment. Damn, they must have gone back to the hotel. No reply.

"Hey, guys, can you hear me?"

Still nothing.

At this time they must be having dinner somewhere. A party to mark the end of the trip with some local officials from the Pokhara region had been organized, and the people who had won races in our tournament would receive medals. Everyone must be out celebrating with the locals. Meanwhile, I was alone, lost in the mountains, in the dark, huddled around my fire—a little point of light glowing in the vast night. The contrast made me smile: a reception full of people, noise, light, music, warmth; a buffet and drinks in the valley below. And here in the mountains above, night, silence, a crackling fire, cold and solitude. Maybe I was better off here. After all, I can't say I'm a party animal, and I'm not really a fan of champagne or award ceremonies. I was content to spend the evening in the company of my fire, with flames dancing for me.

Suddenly, the radio crackled to life again, interrupting the silence.

"JeanDavid, can you hear me? It's François!"

"Finally! Yes, I hear you very clearly."

"I'm out back behind the building, there's good reception here. You know, I just looked up your position on Google Earth—you're twenty kilometres away. It's very strange that the radio signal is working so well."

"What does the map show? Are there any roads?"

"It looks like there's a refuge not too far away, about two hundred metres above your current position."

"Maybe so, but it's impossible for me to get there—the rock rises vertically from where I am. We'll have to find something else."

"Listen, it wasn't possible to send the choppers today, but first thing tomorrow we're coming to get you."

"OK. Are you at the party?"

"Yes. It's strange, really. A bit surreal. Everybody is here, and we're having a good time, and yet we're all thinking of you, imagining you perched up there all alone."

"Reassure them I'm fine, and have fun!"

The voice on the other end changed.

"JeanDavid, it's Laurent. You OK, buddy?"

"Yeah, just a guy spending Friday night on his own while his friends are out partying!"

"We're all thinking of you, you're all we're talking about, you know . . . Use your sail as a blanket. It's airtight, and you can wrap yourself up in it—it ought to protect you from the cold. But try not to sweat so you don't get too cold afterwards."

"I managed to start a fire with the battery of my motor. I'm OK, I'm not so cold now."

"Great! Well, save the battery on your radio—we're gonna need it. If anything comes up, call us, OK? We're staying tuned in and will be listening for you."

"OK, guys, have fun."

There was a short pause.

"JeanDavid, this is François again. I'm not very useful here anymore and I have to be back in Paris on Sunday to help Christine empty her cellar. I'm taking the plane scheduled tomorrow afternoon from Kathmandu to Delhi, then Paris. Let's meet at the airport, OK?"

"Uh, sure, if you want . . . If the choppers come early

enough tomorrow morning, I'll take the first flight to Kathmandu and meet up with you there."

"Great. Take care!"

"Whatever . . ."

I turned off the radio again.

VII

The Night

The thick mist had dissipated and the darkness of night had set in. The fire crackled, lighting my immediate surroundings. I felt its warmth on my face. In the darkness, the glow and sound of the flames created a sort of intimacy. The fire was my companion for now, but not for much longer—I was running low on fuel.

I had to settle down for the night. I was sprawled out on the bag puffed full of the sail—it was relatively comfortable. I stayed that way for a few minutes, keeping close to the fire and watching the sky. In the immense intimacy of that moment, I felt like I was alone in the world, lost between the rock and the stars, filled with joy to be alive and breathing.

I watched the flames dance, listened to the sound of the damp wood as it burned, throwing a trail of sparks into the air as it crackled and popped. One of those sparks almost set the bag on fire!

I had been on the ledge for six or seven hours and hadn't really felt the time pass. I wasn't hungry or thirsty, and I wasn't particularly tired either. There was nothing left to do but wait for sleep. In spite of the fire, which I was trying to get closer to, it was starting to get really cold. I decided to take the sail out of its bag to make a sort of bedding. Spreading it out as best as possible, I wrapped it around me. But it wasn't comfortable at all. The ground, a frozen rock shelf, was cold and hard. The lines tangled and wrapped around my limbs, practically strangling me. I used the harness as a pillow and tried to get into a position to sleep.

But I couldn't shut my eyes. The fire flickered out, and I found myself in the dark. It was pitch black and frigid. I was overcome by a dense, damp and penetrating chill. I curled up, shutting myself inside the airtight sail, using my own breath to warm the pocket of air around my body. But after a few minutes I started to suffocate and had to let in some outside air. Although I managed to warm the air inside the sail a little with my breath, the cold continued to creep up from the ground below. I was chilled to the core. My body started trembling and shivering involuntarily—at first, just at intervals, but then continuously. My teeth chattered, and I twitched and jolted. It was like having a high fever, shivering non-stop even under a pile of blankets. It was impossible to regain control of my own body.

All I could hear was the sound of my own ragged breathing. I had to concentrate on something else. Shaking, I began to recite scales. Major scales first. E-flat major. E-flat, F, G, A-flat, B-flat, C, D, E-flat. I wondered which key I was in. The cold had become so invasive that I couldn't concentrate; I shouted the answers into the dark as though I were throwing off its weight. Soon, I couldn't even get to the end of a scale. I would start over again, louder and louder, trying to finish at least one. The words were becoming impossible to articulate—I couldn't pronounce the words correctly anymore.

I grabbed the radio and tried to turn it on. I had to talk to someone. My hands were shaking so badly, I had trouble turning the knob, but I couldn't get anybody to answer. I curled up again, buried under the sail. Tangled in the lines, I felt like a trussed piece of meat. I concentrated my frustrations on the cords and tried, unsuccessfully, to rip one free from the sail. Then I decided to get out of the sail and do some exercise, push-ups, anything to keep warm. It didn't work. The worst part of the night came around three in the morning. I counted the minutes remaining until sunrise, and each minute seemed like an hour. After a while I lost consciousness and I don't remember . . .

Around five in the morning dawn started to break. First the glow of daylight and then rays of sunlight began to reveal a view that took my breath away.

Finally, the sunlight reached me. I felt as though I was centre stage in an immense, empty theatre, lit by a flood of warming light that slowly enveloped my entire body.

I was dazzled by what lay before me.

And above all, I wasn't cold anymore.

VIII

Morning View

The vision that appeared was sublime. I had never seen anything so extraordinary. Before me, just below my ledge, spread a sea of clouds, and above it, a pure blue sky of the sort you see from an airplane flying above the clouds. From this vast cottony carpet emerged the peaks of the Himalayas, each one more majestic than the last. I was mesmerized.

The sun was shining and rising quickly, its light intensifying steadily. The spectacle changed with each passing minute. I started to warm up and took off my helmet, which hadn't left my head until then. The contrast was striking—the cool air prickled my scalp and made me shiver. The helmet had been keeping me warm. I never wear hats, but I realized then their incredible warming power. I can't even imagine what my night would have been like without the helmet.

I was waiting until 6 a.m. to turn on the radio, thinking my friends must still be asleep, but all of a sudden it crackled. In the delirium of the night, I must have turned it on without switching it off again.

"JeanDavid, are you there?"

"Yes, I am."

"Hi, JeanDavid, this is Stephan. How are you?"

"I've been better!"

"How was your night?"

"Well, I didn't sleep much. Big party here! Very hot girls, drinks, music, you know how it is . . . Tell me about the rescue. What's your plan? Coming with the chopper now?"

"Laurent is on his way to the airport. Chopper team should be ready for takeoff by 7:30."

"If you go through the clouds, visibility here is fantastic. Hurry up. I'm afraid it's going to change."

"Seven thirty is the earliest because before that the airport is closed. You must be hungry."

"Um, not really. I'm OK, actually."

"Well, few people come out alive from sleeping in the Himalayas at 3,000 metres with no equipment in the middle of January."

"Thanks for telling me! Good to know, in case I have to spend another night here!"

"How is the battery of your radio?"

I looked at the symbol showing the charge left. It was still at maximum, which was strange because I'd already used it a fair amount. How could it still be fully charged?

"Seems good."

"You should save it. Turn off the radio, and let's talk in an hour."

"OK."

"JeanDavid?"

"Yes?"

"By 8:00 or 8:30 maximum, you will be saved, and we'll all be together. We'll have breakfast together, OK? By the way, François took a car to Kathmandu this morning. He'll be waiting for you there to catch the plane to Delhi. We already made arrangements for you and booked a flight from Pokhara to Kathmandu later this morning."

"No worries. I'll be here waiting for you guys. I don't really have a choice, do I?"

IX

Cut Off from the World

I still wasn't hungry, but it had been twenty-four hours since I had last eaten, and my mouth was dry. I decided to have some of the chocolate bar in my pocket. I broke off one of the squares, slipped it into my mouth and let it melt on my tongue, closing my eyes and trying to make the most of the moment. It was delicious.

I folded up my sail, stuffed it back in the bag and spread out on top of it facing the sun—this time in full sunbathing mode. After the torture of the night, I eagerly soaked up the warmth and light.

At 7:00 a.m. I decided to switch on the radio again.

When I turned the dial, nothing happened. I didn't understand. Just an hour earlier the battery had been full! How had it gone from maximum charge to dead? I tried again and again, but there was nothing. This was a serious problem; my situation had taken a dramatic turn. Without the radio, I was truly alone.

I tried to find a way to get it to work again. Warming up the batteries did nothing. I tried to rig up an alternative, wiring the battery from the paramotor to the radio, but that didn't work either. The short circuit I had used to start the fire must have drained the motor's battery— when I had first woken up, I'd already tried to start a fire again without managing to generate a spark.

I still had my telephone, which I had turned off when the battery was at 20 percent. This would to be enough to make a few calls and guide a helicopter if one showed up; after all, they had my GPS coordinates.

I turned on the phone. The indicator showed only 4 percent, probably the effect of a night in the cold. iPhones automatically shut off when the battery reaches 2 or 3 percent. I would soon be cut off! I decided to send a few texts.

ME TO GROUND TEAM
Radio just died :(almost no more
bat on phone

NADIA
Hey there! It's Nadia. am in Paris
until Wednesday. R u in Paris?

ALEX
How's it going? I'd love to
get dinner with you
some evening... :)
Take care. Alex

All of my texts from the previous night flooded in. Now was not the time! My phone was going to die any minute.

ME TO GROUND TEAM
I'm alone now :(Hurry up

I wasn't getting anywhere. Without any means of communication, the situation wouldn't be the same at all. How could I be sure that they'd be able to see me from the helicopter? I was just a speck of dust in this vast expanse of mountain. Without a phone or radio, I had no way to guide them in. And nothing with which to start a fire that would be visible from a distance. For the first time, I felt in danger.

ME TO GROUND TEAM
No fire to make fire

ME TO GROUND TEAM
Hurry with choper not sure viz
will stay!!!

The perfect weather of the early morning had begun to change. The clouds thickened; I could see that a helicopter would soon be unable to make it through. Nobody responded to my messages, and I knew I only had a few minutes of battery left.

TRIPIT
Check-in may be avail for AF225
dep DEL 23/1/2011 01:45.
Conf#3IW2IH, MIGVVN http://
www.tripit.com/t/703907e236d8

TripIt is an airport information service that automatically informs you by text message whether your flight is on time. My return flight to Paris that afternoon was confirmed. Good to know!

EFI
THE RESQU TEEM ON THE
WAY

ME TO EFI
*Tell them to bring cigarettes and
lighter*

I was starting to freak out and had a terrible craving for a cigarette. This telecommunication problem wasn't funny at all, and the guys on the ground seemed in no hurry to reply. François had already left town without worrying too much about what would happen to me. Stephan, who was supposed to have taken things in hand, seemed overwhelmed by the situation and had stopped answering. And where was Viktor?

The minutes passed. It was nearly 7:30. The weather was getting worse. It now seemed impossible that a helicopter would manage to make it through the clouds.

ME TO GROUND TEAM
Viz is over! Why didn't you send
chopper earlier?!!

I was far from reassured. Those idiots! They could have taken advantage of this morning's beautiful weather, gotten ready at dawn and come to find me in the helicopter. It had been almost three hours since the sun had risen. They still hadn't done anything, and it was probably too late now. I was losing faith in them. And François leaving me like that . . . I started to get angry.

ME TO GROUND TEAM
If nothing new in 1hr I start to
move

RICHARD
Mon ami, I go to Paris for a sexy
rendez-vous tonight! I need
your help! I must get her out of
the hotel where she is with her
business partner. Where do u
recommend for sexy fun hotel,
my fave (l'hotel) is sold out.

Richard is a good friend. A sometime filmmaker and
the king of burlesque shows, he founded the trendy
New York cabaret The Box. We've had some good times
together in Paris and New York, but I really couldn't
help him just then.
There seemed to be a clearing in the clouds.

ME TO GROUND TEAM
Send choper now viz open!!! If In
one hour nothing
I rescue myself

I had just sent the message when the screen went black.
A little circle appeared and started spinning. Turning off

. . . Please wait.

I had no means of communication whatsoever.

Now I was really alone.

X

Saving Myself

I wasn't about to spend a second night there. Even the idea of it was unbearable after what I'd gone through. If the helicopter didn't show up, I would have to find another solution. It was about 8:00 a.m. Stephan had said that the helicopter would leave around 7:30. It shouldn't take more than fifteen minutes to get to my location from the airport—they had my GPS coordinates; presumably I'd see them coming. The problem would be them finding me. The mountain was so huge . . . How would they spot me?

I realized that my sail should be visible from a distance if I spread it out on the rock. I found a good place where it could lie flat and unfolded it as much as possible. The flash on my camera would allow me to send a visual signal. Luckily, the camera battery was still fully charged, although by that point I was getting wary of batteries.

I waited, on the lookout for the helicopter. The minutes slipped past. Around 8:30, I heard a noise. It had to be the helicopter. It got closer. There it is, I thought, it must be them; I'll see them coming at any moment. When nothing appeared, I started to doubt. Was it really the helicopter I had heard? Not just the whistling wind? Was it my imagination? The noise seemed to fade into the distance. How was this happening? They had my coordinates; they ought to have been there, right in front of me! What the hell were they doing?

I thought I heard the helicopter a second time. I scanned the horizon, the sun in my eyes. A sea of clouds spread endlessly below, the mountaintops piercing through it to my left and a strip of frozen trees and bushes tumbling down the mountainside on my right. The sheer wall behind me stretched high above and might create an echo. The sound faded away. Maybe it was my imagination again. Now it was almost 10:00 a.m., and still nothing.

If they had left at 8:00, they should have arrived ages ago. Something must have happened. Maybe I had got the coordinates wrong; maybe I had misread them or made a mistake in my text. Or maybe I had used the wrong measurement units (my GPS had options for six different systems).

I summed up my situation. On the previous day, the sun had set around 5:00 p.m. It was now 10 a.m. I had seven hours of daylight left. Seven hours might be enough time to get down the mountain if I kept up a good pace.

I set a deadline. If they didn't arrive within the hour, I would find a way to get out of the situation on my own. After all, if I could hike down the mountain, I would eventually come across a village, a road, something. I waited . . .

The idea of saving myself eventually took over. I could do it. I'd find a way out of there, even if it took some time. I was sure to come across a slope that wasn't so steep. The main thing was getting off this wall.

I kept waiting—10:30 a.m., then 11:00 a.m. came and went. The pressure started to rise. The longer I waited, the less time I would have to hike. No way was I spending another night in the cold, and I was sure I could make it down. I wasn't going to stay stuck there, alone, doing nothing. Besides, if they had the wrong coordinates, they would never find me. There was no point in lingering. I was wasting precious time; I had no choice. It was 11:30 and I only had six hours of daylight left—it was already past the deadline I'd set for myself. I couldn't wait any longer, so I started out.

XI

Getting Off the Ledge

I couldn't take all of my equipment with me. I had to make some choices. There was no way to carry the motor—far too heavy. The bag for the sail had straps like a backpack and seemed manageable, but it would be too bulky; given the kind of terrain I was about to climb across, it would get in the way more than anything. And besides, I wouldn't need it—I wasn't going to spend another night in the mountains. It would probably be more useful spread out and visible from a distance. I could take the rest of my things in my fanny pack.

Having decided to leave the ledge where I had spent the night and go down the mountain on my own filled me with optimism. I was enthusiastic to set off on this adventure. It couldn't be that difficult. A bit of rock climbing followed by a walk down the mountain, and it would be over—I was just going on a sort of hike. Trekking wasn't really my thing, but I could make the best of it, get some exercise and enjoy the scenery. I knew I would miss my 1:45 flight but, oh well, I thought, that's life. There was surely another flight later in the evening. Well, maybe that evening was stretching it, but I could definitely shoot for a flight the following morning.

I gave my motor one last look, realizing I would probably never see it again. I was attached to that machine—we had shared a fair number of adventures. I thought of our flights in Syria, Croatia, Greece, Ibiza, the United States, Israel, Malaysia . . . It was a compact, reliable motor, always trustworthy, always ready for takeoff. We were well-suited to each other. Sure, it shook a little and was a bit heavy, but it was easy to travel with, powerful, and quick to set up. My sail was precious too. I had bought it in Israel; Jimmy had helped me choose it. It was good for easy takeoffs and fast flying. But sail designs change often, and sails have to be replaced regularly for safety reasons. Mine had taken quite a beating, and it was on its last legs anyway. Then I looked at the black and mauve sail bag that Jimmy had given me, made from a vibrant fabric that I had never seen anywhere else. I would miss that too. It was too big to take along. I had to travel light.

I considered all of the possible paths leading away from the ledge. To my left was a sheer cliff. On my right the slope was very steep, nearly vertical. A few rocks and bushes, barely reachable, protruded from the mountain-side. But I had to find a trail. I looked ahead a little, and about two hundred metres in the distance, I could see a patch of trees. Where there are trees, there is always something to hold on to—roots, branches. I couldn't see past them, but it seemed like the slope grew less steep. It might even be practicable. I had to go in that direction.

A nearly vertical wall towered above me. The steep facade just barely allowed me to remain standing, but there was no margin for error. If I missed a step, I would fall, and it would be impossible to catch myself. One by one, I searched for new footings and handholds. I was moving slowly. With no equipment, I had only the strength in my hands and arms to depend on. I tested everything I might grip—bushes, roots, holes, rocks—before I put my weight on them. Arm over arm, leg after leg, I found myself in the middle of a steep field of stones.

It took me over an hour to make it across the 200 metres to the trees. Toward the end, I had gradually shifted from rock climbing to a sort of controlled scramble. But I had been right about the trees. Once among them, I could move from trunk to trunk by holding on to the branches, edging down the mountain. I eventually arrived at a more approachable patch of terrain with a gentler slope. This was a good sign. I leaned back and let myself slide down the slope, spreading out my legs and arms, dragging my hands and feet to keep from going too fast. After about fifteen metres, the slope eased up further, and I could stand. Finally, I could walk.

All I had to do now was follow the slope down the mountain. I was home free! I had gotten past the worst, now I just had to walk down. Soon, I was sure to come across a road or a village, something man-made. The nightmare was over! It was a beautiful day. I was warm. I had pulled it off. I was elated.

Now it was just a hike in the woods.

XII

Going Down the Mountain

The ice that covered almost everything at a higher altitude gradually disappeared as I descended, giving way to stone fields scattered with trees and bushes. Making progress still wasn't easy, and the slope grew steeper again. Most of the time, I had to slide on the seat of my pants.

Little by little the landscape started to change. The vegetation grew denser and became a true forest with trees, ferns and clumps of different kinds of plants. And then it became jungle. A jungle is terrible—there is no way to go forward without pushing through branches and bushes or being scratched by thorns. Sometimes the canopy of the trees overhead was so dense that it blocked out the sky.

All of a sudden, I heard a noise—the hum of an approaching helicopter. I froze. The wind in the trees made it difficult to distinguish the sound with certainty. Maybe they were trying to find me. I took out my camera and started setting off the flash toward the sky, thinking my rescuers might see it. Then I stopped to listen again. The noise was moving away. Or maybe it was just my imagination. I listened. I began to think it was just the sound of the wind blowing through the trees. I wasn't sure of anything anymore. What the hell. I started walking again. I knew I had to keep going.

By 3:00 p.m. I had been walking for nearly four hours, with nothing to eat or drink for over thirty hours, apart from one square of chocolate. I could hear my stomach rumble, but oddly, I wasn't hungry or even thirsty. My mouth and throat were dry, my lips were completely chapped, and my tongue had grown hard. I felt my throat burn with each inhalation. I knew I had to find something to drink—I couldn't eat anything before I found some water. With so much exercise at such a high altitude, I knew that each breath was dehydrating me a little more. I also knew that the human body wasn't endlessly forgiving. I had to take care of myself. I hadn't slept. If I didn't eat and drink, I'd eventually fall over. I began looking for water. Only then would I treat myself to a second piece of chocolate.

I spotted a puddle. The water was stagnant and didn't look drinkable, but I had to at least wet my mouth. It was impossible to drink with my hands—the water slipped through my fingers. I tried again and again, but the little water that stayed in my hands only flowed down the inside of my sleeves when I tried to drink.

I couldn't lap at the puddle like an animal, and besides, given the situation, I had no intention of swallowing. I had to find something to hold the water. I looked through my things and saw my GoPro sports camera inside its protective plastic case. I took it apart, and bingo! The case was watertight. Once opened it made the perfect cup. I rinsed my mouth, swirling the water around as though I had just brushed my teeth. It did me good and gave me some relief, though my throat was still raw.

As I continued my descent, I soon heard the sound of flowing water. This time it was a spring—it was music to my ears. I hurried over to see that the spring lay out of reach at the bottom of a precipice. To get to it, I would have to climb down, holding on to branches and roots. It took me nearly half an hour to descend the twenty or twenty-five metres that separated me from the water, and several times, I almost slipped and fell to the floor of the ravine below.

When I finally got to the stream, I flung myself down and drank my fill of the marvellous water that flowed from the very belly of the mountain. I had been proud of my improvised cup, but what counted now was quenching my thirst, soothing my burning throat. I drank until I couldn't drink any more, as if the spring might suddenly dry up and disappear. The water had a funny brackish taste, but I didn't think much of it until my stomach began to hurt. I got suspicious again and stopped drinking. I figured it might be the lack of food—the effect of an empty stomach suddenly filled— but I didn't want to push it, so I continued by just rinsing my mouth and spitting the water. My tongue started to feel normal again, and my throat hurt a little less.

I could at last allow myself a meal and enjoy a second piece of chocolate. I would save the third square for later. I looked for a place where I could sit, take a little break and enjoy my feast. I moved my hand to the pocket where I had put the chocolate bar earlier in the day, but it was already open. I had probably forgotten to zip it shut, or the zipper had gotten hooked on a branch and pulled open on its own. I reached inside, but the chocolate was gone.

I had nothing left to eat.

XIII

Realizing My Mistake

How was I to keep going without anything to eat, especially given all of the energy I had been expending? Three little squares of chocolate weren't much to begin with, but losing them was a completely different story. It was 3:30 p.m. Instead of stopping to wring my hands, I pushed myself to move on. I had to keep going to make it back home.

The mountainside grew steeper again, and I couldn't remain standing. I went back to sliding on the seat of my pants. A noise started to get louder and louder and turned out to be another stream. I was in luck—I figured that if I followed the stream, it would eventually lead to a river that might take me in the correct direction. A river would flow into the valley and join bigger rivers that would eventually flow to the ocean. It had to be the right way to go.

As I continued, the stream grew wider. It was much warmer in the bottom of the ravine, and I was still wearing my helmet, a full-body motorcycle suit and three sweaters. I took off the layers from my upper body to cool off a bit in the spring water. Although I had been able to wade in the stream when I first found it, it soon became a creek flowing over stones and around boulders. I jumped from rock to rock to make my way. They were covered in slippery green moss, and I nearly twisted my ankle.

The riverbanks gradually became steep cliffs, and I found myself trapped in the bottom of a canyon. The current had gotten faster and transformed into rapids that took a sharp turn in the distance. I couldn't make out what came next, but it was clear I couldn't continue; the river had become too rough. I needed to find an alternative route. I had to retrace my steps.

It hadn't been easy following the river down the mountain, but climbing back up was even harder. I had to scramble over slippery obstacles, often climbing on all fours. Sometimes I had to turn back and try another way up. I spent an unimaginable amount of time trying to get past the places I had just jumped over or let myself fall into on the way down. Each boulder became a challenge to overcome; every obstacle tested my will to continue.

I had to get out of the riverbed and back to higher ground. Should I climb the bank to my left or my right? How was I to know? I chose at random. I figured I would just keep going to the right, the direction I had already been heading down the mountain.

I scrambled, climbed and finally made it up the slope. The struggle was exhausting, and I was way too hot. With effort, I got myself up onto the bank and out of the riverbed and started back down the mountain, hoping I wouldn't find myself on the edge of a cliff. Soon, I could see the landscape below open up. I kept moving, slowly. After a while longer, I could see the river I had followed dropping into a hundred-foot waterfall, impossible to cross. Before me, another empty drop. A cliff. A dead end. Opposite lay a valley followed by another gigantic mountain. Mountain upon mountain, I was surrounded.

Suddenly everything started spinning. I held my head in my hands as I felt a horrible sensation come over me. I dropped to my knees. I realized what I had done. I had made a mistake that might cost me my life.

XIV

Anger

I ranted. I hated myself.

I had just figured out that there was not going to be any village, road or house "at the bottom of the mountain"—there would be no ski lodge or cozy restaurant at the end of this trail. Just a valley, followed by other mountains, each one higher, steeper and more daunting than the last. I had made a terrible mistake. The Himalayas are the highest mountain range in the world, over a thousand kilometres long and hundreds of kilometres wide, with most of the mountains uninhabited. How could I have possibly expected to come across a village? I had walked into a giant trap.

I had no sense of direction; my GPS wasn't loaded with local maps. I didn't know what point I had come down from, and I had no idea where Pokhara might be situated. I was completely surrounded by peaks. If I kept going, I could just as easily be travelling deeper into the Himalayas. I had crawled, slid and scrambled down slopes and over obstacles that I could never climb back over again. It was impossible to locate my starting point. By deciding to leave the ledge where I had spent the night, I had voluntarily sent myself into oblivion.

Had I stayed in one place, the rescuers would have had a chance of finding me. They had my GPS coordinates, even if they were slightly off. From the ledge on the mountain, I would have spotted the helicopter—they would have been able to see my sail. In my current position, I was lost in the depths of the forest, in the middle of nowhere. It would be impossible to find me.

What in the world had driven me to leave the spot where the rescuers knew I was waiting for them? How could I have had the audacity to believe that I could make it out on my own just by "going down the mountain"?

I was furious. I hated myself for having made such a serious decision without taking the time to properly think it over. To die in a violent fall, a crash, an accident is terrible, of course, but an accident is an accident. Dying from a lack of common sense, from impatience or because you think you can "do it by yourself," dying because of a spur-of-the-moment decision just seemed stupid. "Here lies JeanDavid, he was too sure of himself" or "he was in a hurry" or "he was a fool." Dying alone, lost in the mountains.

How would I make it back to civilization? I was angry, that's for sure. Angry at myself, my recklessness, my idiocy, my insolence. I cursed the thin air. I told myself that if God existed and wanted to send me a message, he had just done so. Fate had saved me from the worst at the moment of my crash, and I had thrown all that away.

"What an IDIOT!" I repeated over and over, raging in circles. I tried to calm down, but I couldn't shake my own anger. If something happened to me now, I was entirely responsible, me and my idiot brain.

The worst was that I didn't give a damn about death—I was convinced I wouldn't suffer. Exhausted, cold and hungry, I would probably go in my sleep, a peaceful slumber from which I simply wouldn't wake up. I'd had a good life. If things ended here, so be it. Besides, we all have to die sometime.

But what about my daughter? My parents? They'd be eaten up with grief.

I couldn't do that to them.

XV

Taking Responsibility

I had to stop wasting my energy on pointless anger. I tried to calm down. Being angry served no purpose—allowing my fury to get the better of me would just add stupidity to an already foolish decision.

I began walking again, heading back up the slope to avoid the edge of the cliffs. The physical exertion helped me focus and gather my wits. Was I afraid? I gave it some thought and realized that, no, strangely, I wasn't afraid—not at all. I was angry, but when you're in the moment, you don't feel fear. Only the unknown, or the idea of the unknown, stirs up fear. When you're face-to-face with your problem, it's no longer an unknown.

I thought about my daughter and my parents. I had to be responsible. Responsible for myself, responsible toward my family and my friends. In part, their grief or their happiness was in my hands. My error might now inflict pain and sadness on them, and the very idea of this was unbearable.

I hoped that Rebecca hadn't tried to get in touch with me, but at the same time I wasn't too concerned. She was more preoccupied with her friends, her BlackBerry and her Facebook account than with her father's flying adventures. Kids her age call their parents to placate them or to ask for something. Of course, eventually she'd start to worry, because I never let more than forty-eight hours go by without calling to find out what she was up to—we talked on almost every even-numbered day. But that rule was starting to slip. In the beginning I tried to call her out on it, but then I remembered the way I communicated with my parents when I was a teenager. I had come to understand the careful discretion with which my parents had waited for my occasional need to communicate, because as a father, I now waited for those same signs myself.

Becoming a father means feeling a greater sense of responsibility. I felt the need to tell Rebecca these things. I had to tell her, to try to explain. I wanted her to understand that I had made a terrible mistake, made the wrong decision, taken useless risks. But I also needed her to know that mistakes are part of life, part of one's destiny. I didn't want her to be sad. I wanted her to know that I loved her. That my death had certainly come unexpectedly soon, but that this was the way of the world, and that she should continue to make the most of her life, now more than ever. My parents would be grieving, too, and she should stand by them because they would need her.

I wanted to tell her all of those things while I was thinking them, while I was still coherent and relatively presentable. If they found my body, at least my message might reach her, leaving her some advice to help her cope, something to help her understand what had happened. I stopped walking and took out my camera, changed the setting to "video" and, holding it at arm's length, in one take, recorded my message for Rebecca.

When I had finished, I stayed seated, gazing off into the distance.

I wondered how things might turn out if I didn't make it back to civilization. What would the end of my life be like, lost in the forest? At what point should I give up trying to make it back alive? How long could I survive? I could easily imagine building a shelter and adjusting to my surroundings. The problem was food. What would I eat? How could I eat it without fire? And what would my friends and family do once I was gone?

It was almost 5:00 p.m. Night would soon fall. In twelve hours it would be two days since I had eaten or slept. I was exhausted from so much high-altitude exertion. I probably wouldn't be able to think clearly for much longer. I knew what that felt like. I had gone all day without eating anything before. You don't think straight after a while. It's a gentle sort of feeling, actually. Thoughts come more slowly, often repetitively. I had to make some simple rules that I could repeat to myself when I became too exhausted to do otherwise.

I made two rules:

Never stop.

And keep my helmet on.

XVI

Finding My Way

I had to keep moving. I had to find a way out, no matter what. But in which direction? If only I had a clear destination. Even with obstacles in your path, traps, barriers, holes, cliffs, you keep fighting to reach a goal. Not knowing where to go or how to concentrate my efforts, I felt like a hamster in a cage running on its wheel leading nowhere. Like a mouse in a maze, scurrying down one hallway after another, trying every hole and path.

The real problem lay in having realized this. Sometimes it's better not to know the truth or see where you stand. Before my epiphany, I was already a mouse in a maze, but

I kept moving forward, light-heartedly braving dangers, climbing slopes, scaling the mountain, crossing rushing rapids. It had been complicated, risky and difficult, but I hadn't known it was futile.

Now that I had seen the vast wilderness in which I was lost, I realized how impossible escape really was. The hopes of coming across a road or a village seemed very slim indeed. I understood that my struggle served no purpose. I had discovered that I was fighting for nothing. Not only had I not moved toward my escape, I had been moving away from it, pushing it into the distance.

Stranded on the mountain ledge, I still had a tangible goal, a way out—I just had to try to survive and wait for a rescue.

Now I waited for nobody. I had nothing. I was only forging deeper into oblivion without knowing why. Or rather, knowing why, but also knowing that I had no direction, no destination, no end in sight. What was the point of doggedly pushing on?

Yet strangely, in spite of all of these realizations, I hadn't lost hope. Faced with the impossibility of climbing back up the mountain, I could only go down. And if going downward took me to another obstacle, I would go around it. In a certain sense, I had no choice. It turned out that my path had been chosen for me, so the lack of decisions to be made didn't distress me. I just had to keep moving on. The rest was fate. The effort and responsibility of moving forward were mine, and it was up to destiny to grant me the thread that would lead me out of the labyrinth. What else could I do, apart from continuing onward? I had to keep moving in order to keep my hope alive.

I had finally found my way.

I would go down the mountain without knowing.

XVII

An Encounter with Nature

I moved forward without stopping. Climbing across rock faces, making my way around boulders, holding on to branches—in a word, going down the mountain to reach the valley. If I was going to be lucky enough to find a road or a footpath, it had to be down there.

As I proceeded, the mouth of a cave came into view between the rocks further ahead. As I got closer, it was still impossible to see inside it. People said there were bears and lynxes in the mountains around Pokhara. I didn't care. After all, I was already lost. I didn't think I was also going to get attacked. I'm not the sort of person who provokes animals, and I couldn't imagine one throwing itself at me for no reason. Besides, I thought, if I encountered an animal, I would just see how things went. I vaguely remembered that bears couldn't climb trees. And if I ran into a lynx, it would probably be more afraid than I was. An encounter might even take my mind off things.

I was near a waterfall and knew I would have to get beyond it to continue my descent. I heard a noise, and I looked up to see a doe and its fawn step from the under-brush. They had come to drink at the stream. A ray of sunlight fell on them, framed in the vegetation, their images reflected in the water. The light was stunning; the whole scene was magical, straight out of *Bambi*.

I froze and watched, moved by the scene. They stepped forward quietly and drank the cool water, pausing to look around peacefully. It almost seemed as though they were smiling at me. I was in their world. I smiled back at them and at nature in general, at the beauty of the spec-tacle of life that was unfolding all around me.

Then a thought crossed my mind. What if hunger drove me to hunt? What would I be capable of doing in the name of survival? I gave up these thoughts pretty quickly as I didn't even have a knife or a way to make a fire. Hunting wasn't an issue yet, and I preferred it that way.

I had to keep going. I changed course, moving away from the waterfall to avoid falling into another ravine.

Once again, I worked my way up, pulling myself from one root and rock to another. Most of the time I was on all fours. When I was on a higher level, I always kept to the right, trying to avoid the edge of the cliffs. In spite of this, my path kept leading back to the brink. I moved forward a few metres at a time, slowly, but I never stopped.

In the distance, I could hear a new noise. I held my breath and listened, trying to focus. It seemed to be the thwack-thwack-thwack of a helicopter. Yes, I was sure I could hear it getting closer. I knew I couldn't miss it this time. I hurried toward a clearing where I could glimpse the sky and have a chance of being seen. I took out the camera, set up the flash and signalled with it once, twice, three times, ten times, hoping that somebody would see the bursts of light below them. I paused and listened again. No, it had only been the wind in the trees. A hallucination. My imagination. I had heard a helicopter flying overhead the way people see mirages in the desert.

I headed back down the mountain, pushing deep into the jungle.

XVIII

A Night in Business Class

My path led me to the edge of the cliffs once again. I had to work my way back up the slope, but it was impossible to walk upright. Night was falling, and I crawled along until I couldn't see anymore. I stopped and felt around for a place to lie down that wouldn't be too hard on my back. The ground was covered in stones.

This time I knew what to expect. I knew that I had ten hours of complete darkness ahead of me during which I would suffer extreme cold. Ten hours. Six hundred minutes. And I didn't have a fire or my sail this time. I was defenseless. I tried to think of something, a way to protect myself, but I came up with nothing. I was completely exposed in the middle of the wilderness. The previous night I had been up on the side of the mountain on a rock ledge. Now I was in the middle of the forest. What if there were spiders, a snake, a large animal? But there was nothing I could do if there were. My main concern was the cold. Waiting for hours, chilled to the core, until the sun rose again. Hours of shivering, uncontrollable shaking. Ten hours. Longer than a flight from Paris to New York.

I thought that if I managed to fall asleep, I might be able to escape the present. I curled up on the ground in the dark, but the cold kept me awake. I got the idea to force myself to relax. I had to calm down completely and take control of my own body. I took slow, deep breaths and ordered my muscles to stop quivering. I had to accept the cold, not struggle against it or try to counter its power. Or perhaps I had to treat the cold by embracing it. I tried to completely loosen my limbs and fuse my body with the rocks and earth; I tried to be one with my environment. Gradually, I began to feel a little less cold, or rather, I could still feel the cold, but I suffered less. My thoughts could wander. Little by little, my muscles relaxed, and I entered a sleep-like state.

I heard a beep. Then a second one. There was some movement. The quiet little sounds you hear in airplanes when the cabin crew is preparing the plane for takeoff.

When a few last passengers come aboard and put their luggage in the overhead bins. When someone rings for the flight attendant with the button on his armrest. It was warm. A warmth both dry and damp, due to the pressurization of the cabin before takeoff.

"Champagne, sir? Water or juice?" a flight attendant asked as she passed, surprised to see me already stretched out and ready to doze off.

"No, thanks. I'm probably just going to sleep right away."

"We're going to take off soon, so you'll have to put your seat back in the upright position, but I promise that I won't wake you again afterwards," she said in an almost maternal tone.

I was reclining in a sleeping position in business class on an Air France flight back to Paris, curled up, my body almost completely under the blanket, my seat belt attached over the top where the flight attendants could see it. I was warm, and my muscles grew heavy. I felt good. It was almost as if I was a child, curled up with the comforter pulled up to my ears, not only because it was warm, but because it felt so good.

I remained motionless, dreaming of that moment, the moment when I would return home stretched out in the warmth, my head on a pillow, protected by the blanket, by the flight attendant, by Air France.

If I made it out of the mountains, I had to take that flight in business class, the seat on the left side of the centre of the plane, next to the aisle. I would hug the flight attendant when she offered me a glass of champagne. That flight home would be the sweetest moment. When I got home I would go to my bathroom and take a long hot shower that would never end.

I made a date with myself on that flight.

XIX

A Hole in the Night

The cold took the upper hand and I was wracked with trembling again. I knew I couldn't stay on the ground. I had to do something; I had to move my body. Hadn't I made it a rule never to stop? Well, now was the time to keep going. At least the exertion would warm me up. The night was pitch-black, for although the moon had started rising, it was still hidden by the trees overhead. I could make out the shadows of the boulders, trees and other obstacles that lay around me. I took my iPod from the fanny pack and turned it on. It read 11:00 p.m. I held it between my teeth and used it as a flashlight. It only stayed on for thirty seconds at a time, but that was long enough to make out the next outline, the next handhold. To move forward and climb the slope, I had to stay on all fours, always pausing to turn on the iPod again. I ended up continuing in the dark, feeling the ground with my hands. After all, it wasn't speed that mattered, just movement. I needed to stay warm.

Suddenly, my hand gave way, and I fell into what seemed to be a hole. I had thought I was reaching for a root, but I had groped thin air. With my other hand I held on tight to a root. My legs swung in the air, trying to find a foothold. I couldn't see below me to make out whether it was an empty void or just a slight change in elevation. I didn't know where I was. I felt around with my other hand until I found something to hold on to and pulled myself up with all my strength, strength that I never knew I possessed. I had pulled with so much force that I managed to get back up to solid ground with what felt like little effort. I fell back, breathless. I definitely wasn't cold anymore.

I kept moving forward cautiously, making sure each step was safe. My eyes grew accustomed to the dark. Rays of moonlight started to seep through the treetops. I moved at a slow, steady pace, never stopping.

Day began to break. I must have crawled hundreds of metres in the night. I had climbed far from the cliffs. I knew I had to keep moving around them. A little higher up the slope I could make out a break in the trees. What was it? Another line of cliffs? A way down? A field? It was still too far away, so I kept crawling forward, climbing up the mountain. I was exhausted. With a little more effort I knew I could reach the clearing, and maybe from there I could see something. The previous day I had stayed mostly deep in the brambles and underbrush of the forest and had had no real landmarks to orient myself. Now I could see that there was indeed a break in the trees. I could see the mountain across the valley, the mountains all around. It was expansive and beautiful, but I wasn't any further along.

Then a detail suddenly leapt out at me. Nothing had changed and yet everything had changed. In the distance, hidden deep in the flank of the mountain across the valley, I could make out a form that seemed unnatural, an area that was slightly greener than the rest, a geometrical form, a rectangle that clearly wasn't wilderness. It was a field, a plot of farmed land. It had to be. Whatever it was, it had to be man-made. And if it was man-made, there had to be a road leading from it, a path of some sort, a trail that would lead me back to civilization. If I could reach it, it would be the beginning of my road home.

I had lost all contact with humankind, and yet here in this vast expanse of wilderness lay the miraculous trace of man's labour. I held the thread that would lead me out of the labyrinth.

XX

A Leap of Faith

Nevertheless, I still wasn't out of harm's way. The field was at least fifteen kilometres away, and in the mountains it's not the distance that determines how long the journey will be. But I had a goal now, and that changed everything. I was no longer the mouse in a maze: The way out was in sight.

Yet it was impossible for me to go straight toward the field. The edge of the cliff still waited below. I had to move around it again. I scanned the landscape, trying to distinguish the path that would lead me to my field and back to civilization. I memorized the surrounding terrain, scanning the lay of the land all the way up to the highest visible points. The field lay at the foot of two peaks, separated by a plateau. They would be my landmark. To the right of where I stood, a path led down the mountain—while not a gentle slope, at least it seemed accessible. To get to my field I had to keep bearing to the right. It was 6:00 a.m., and I had the whole day ahead of me. I set out with determination.

Having an objective to reach for after going so long without one was like passing from cold to warmth, from darkness to light, from depression to euphoria. My strength multiplied tenfold. I moved quickly and, although I hadn't eaten and had hardly slept in three days, I felt no hunger or fatigue.

As I continued through the forest, I started to lose my bearings. I simply hoped I was still going in the right direction. I tried to keep the mountains in view whenever possible, and I was always on the lookout for the two peaks. Of course, as my trail continued downward, they gradually disappeared. But I remained confident.

I kept moving down the mountain. When I reached areas that were too sheer to climb down, I walked back up again. Over and over again. Each time I came to a steep spot, I hoped I wouldn't fall into the abyss. Once, the top of a tree was almost in reach. Grabbing hold of it would save me from going back up the slope. I hesitated, thinking I might jump and let the branches cushion my fall, but I abandoned the idea, afraid I might hurt myself.

It would have been a pity to break a bone when I was so close to my goal. So I kept moving back up and around the steep patch, before heading back down again.

When the slope grew even steeper, I slid seated, trying not to go too fast. Sliding down, I found myself on the edge of a drop-off and stopped just in time. The next patch of solid ground below me seemed near enough, but when I tried to edge closer, I found it wasn't reachable. I could hold on to a root, dangle and let myself fall. I grabbed the root, turned around and let go. But I had underestimated the distance. The branches below had hidden the facts, and I landed on a ledge just a few centimetres wide, hanging above a precipice.

There was no way back up. The root I had used to swing down was out of reach now. The ledge I was standing on receded into the rock face on either side. Below, there was nothing to hold on to or lean against. An empty void stretched out before me, and the ground was at least ten or twelve metres below. There was no way out. I had to jump.

Nine metres is the height of a three-storey building. I couldn't see what was further below, but it was probably a steep slope leading to another drop-off. I was stuck. There was no way up, no way down, no way out on either side. It wasn't possible to climb out or even sit down. I found myself standing, my back to the wall, looking out over the abyss as if condemned to walk the plank.

I would surely break something if I jumped. For the moment, though, I was still in one piece. For how long? It was a strange feeling. Usually, we don't bring accidents upon ourselves—sometimes we see them coming and try to avoid the worst, but we don't walk into them voluntarily. This was exactly the opposite situation. I had no way of avoiding what was about to happen, but I was free to decide when it would take place. There would be a before and an after. In the before, I was in one piece; in the after, I would be broken, a direct result of my own decision. It's not easy to tell yourself, "Go on, now's the moment. Jump and break something."

But I had to keep moving. I couldn't spend the night there.

Just as I was about to jump, I held myself back, thinking that there must be a better way than breaking a random limb. At this point in the journey, my legs were more important than my arms. I had to be able to keep walking. And if I had to land on an arm, it should be my left arm, because I'm right-handed. But either arm would do, really, as long as it wasn't a foot, a leg, or a hip.

Go on, I thought, jump . . . I couldn't torture myself any longer. The time was now.

I got into position. By instinct, perhaps, instead of jumping, I turned and let myself slide down the rock face, trying to hold on with my hands, fingers and nails, like a cat using its claws. I gained a few metres, and then I fell into the emptiness.

A branch sticking out from the cliff whacked me in the head like a blow from a club. I continued to tumble down, rolled up into a ball. I hit the ground at full speed and bounced off the side of the wall. The base of my spine smashed into a jutting root. I lay motionless, in shock. I was conscious and in pain, unable to move.

I was stunned.

XXI

Don't Stop, Ever

Without the helmet I would have cracked my head open. It had already protected me from the cold, and now it had saved my life. I was groggy, but my head didn't hurt. The pain was strongest on my right side at the base of my back. The wind had been knocked out of me. I thought that, after a fall like that, my spine was probably damaged. I waited a few minutes before trying to appraise my condition.

I started by moving the fingers of my right hand, then those of my left hand. They worked. Then I moved my arms—they reacted normally. The muscles ached, but I could move. But what about my legs? Could I move them? I paused a long moment before finding the courage to test them. I was terrified of being paralyzed. I stared at my right leg. "Go on, please tell me you still work," I thought. If I could just move it, even a little bit, I'd be fine. It might be broken, hurt, damaged, but at least I wouldn't be paralyzed. I tried to move it just a tiny bit. Yes! It moved! And rather well! I tried the left leg, and it was the same. I closed my eyes and breathed a sigh of relief. Slowly, I uncurled my body and lay on the ground next to the root. I extended my legs and stretched, spreading my arms. There was pain in my lower back, but I was in one piece.

Little by little, I started to stir. My limbs were stiff, but they responded. I couldn't afford to dawdle, so I got up. Don't stop, ever.

I had trouble walking. My back hurt, and I limped. Yet I had to crawl through brambles and bushes. I persisted, crawling for hours without stopping.

My head started to spin. I was getting tired. I could feel my thoughts slowing. It was as though I had been drained of all my strength. I couldn't think anymore. I kept on moving like a stubborn animal, stumbling, climbing upward, teetering along the edge of the cliff, not allowing myself any rest for fear of not getting up again. "Don't stop, ever."

I was exhausted. I hadn't seen my two peaks for a long time, and I no longer knew where I was. But I had to continue. "Don't stop, ever." I repeated those words, over and over, like some corny tune.

When I needed to rest, I would slow down slightly, but I refused to stop moving. I kept on, my muscles numb, almost at a standstill, advancing centimetre by centimetre. After three days of exertion, several nights without sleeping and no food, the thing you crave most is rest. But I refused to sit down. I fought against the fatigue. I wouldn't stop until I reached my goal. One step. Then another. And again, starting over. "Don't stop, ever." It had become an obsession.

Then I noticed something on the ground—some sort of animal dropping. It was huge—the animal must be enormous. A bear? The dung was dry and seemed several days old. Perhaps I had stumbled upon a bear's territory?

I came across a second dropping. Then a third. They were fresher. I slowed down and listened, but I heard nothing. I picked up my pace. Suddenly, I heard something moving in a bush ahead of me. I surprised myself by shouting, "Anybody there?" What else do you say in a situation like that? It was the best thing I could think of to get a reaction.

I kept walking, and the sound started up again. I was trying to figure out where it came from when I spotted a cow.

It was nice to see another living being! I started talking to it.

"You wouldn't happen to know a way out of here,

would you?" She looked at me, motionless. She seemed surprised.

"Come on, be cool and show me the way!"

She turned around and another cow appeared. This one was wearing a bell! That meant they weren't wild, they might be part of a herd that had been set loose to graze. There had to be a farm.

As I headed up another slope, I saw sunlight through the trees.

The hill seemed insurmountable—I had come so many kilometres, but I was hitting a physical wall. I forced myself to trudge the last metre or so that separated me from the clearing. I saw more cows. I walked closer. They were wearing bells too. I walked past them and reached the last trees, drained of energy. Beyond them, the view opened up, and the slope became more manageable. I looked out into the distance.

About five kilometres away, at the bottom of the hill, I could see my rectangle.

XXII

Making It Through

There was more than just the field. I could see some buildings too. And movement—it was definitely movement. I stepped beyond the edge of the forest to be more visible and started shouting.

"Heeeellp! Maaaayday! French pilot! Heeellp!"

I shouted at the top of my lungs.

"Heeeeeeelp!"

I took out my camera and started setting off the flash. Suddenly, I heard somebody shouting in return. I didn't understand anything, but I replied, screaming my head off.

"Lost French piiiiilot! Heeeelp me pleeeease!"

I tried to understand what they were shouting back,

but it was impossible. Since the words didn't mean anything, I shifted strategies. I decided it wasn't what I said that counted, it was just a question of making a number of sounds in succession. I shouted once, then a second time and a third. Then silence. After a few moments I heard the same number of sounds in return. I had been heard. They knew where I was. I was saved!

This time, never mind the holes, the crevices, the ravines, the precipices separating me from the field, I was going down that hill in a straight line. Nothing could convince me to take another path. I was going straight ahead.

I felt like a robot going full speed. I couldn't feel my legs anymore. I rushed down the slope, jumping over obstacles in my path, running down banks through the brambles and bushes. The fatigue started to catch up with me as I went, and several times I almost fell, but I started walking again. Those last few kilometres were interminable; the field was still impossibly far away. I had underestimated the distance.

I had been moving for an hour or two when, to my left, about thirty metres away, I saw two men coming up the slope at a clip—they were clearly in a hurry. They were the first human beings I had seen in three days. I wasn't going to let them get away!

"Hey!"

They saw me and looked at each other questioningly before continuing on their way up the hill.

"Heeey! Help me!"

They stopped again, looked beyond me into the distance and then stared at me, disconcerted.

"Yes! That's me! I'm the French pilot!"

In their hurry to reach me, they had probably imagined that I was still in the place from where I had shouted and set off my flash, thinking that I wouldn't budge from there. But since then, almost two hours had passed, I'd moved . . .

They exchanged a few words and then hurried to my side, shouting with joy, clearly happy to have found me. They took me in their arms. They didn't want to let go of me. I didn't want those men to let go either, even though I had never seen them before. They were poor, elderly Nepali farmers, something out of another time and civilization. But they were my rescuers. I hugged them tight, terrified of losing them.

Tears flowed from my eyes. I couldn't help it, but I didn't want them to see. I tried to hold in my sobs, but it was impossible. I thought of my daughter, my parents, my family, my friends. This rescue had saved them from grief and pain. All of the terrible consequences I had imagined, the video testament for Rebecca, all that vanished in an instant. I was going to go home, see my friends, continue my old life . . . Back to civilization, the city, cars, noise, the telephone, Internet, daily life in Paris. Nobody would need to know. Nobody would need to know, because nobody needed to suffer. Maybe I'd tell them—probably, but in the way you tell a story. The way you talk about "something cool" that happened to you. All of these thoughts hit me at once.

What I had just lived through, those three days alone in the mountains, suddenly lost all semblance of reality. I felt like I was leaving a movie theatre: I was a bit disoriented, the film was over, and although my mind was still in the story, my hands were already rummaging through my pockets for my car keys. Life was shifting back to normal. What had just happened was becoming fiction. It was a strange feeling.

I wanted to take the road to the field immediately. I tried to make the men understand that I wanted to go down the hill—and go home. We still had a good hour and a half of walking ahead of us.

As we walked, mental images of my journey came rushing back in reverse order: the cow, my fall, the waterfall, the spring, the fire on the mountain ledge in the cold. It already seemed so far away. I saw in my mind the movie of what had just happened to me, with the impression of not having lived through it myself.

At a turn in the road, we came upon five other men. They had probably set out along with my rescuers, but my two Nepali farmers were much faster, even in sandals, and they seemed to know the area better. One of the newcomers had brought food and water. Another had a telephone.

A third spoke English. I was now clearly out of danger. They offered me some crackers, but I wasn't hungry. I tried to eat a few, but I couldn't swallow. It wasn't my throat; I just didn't have any appetite. I drank a little. The man with the telephone was having a lively conversation with the person on the other end. He seemed proud and happy. There was no need to speak Nepali to understand. The phone kept ringing. I took a few photos. But I mostly wanted to keep moving, to go back. It was past five and night was falling. I motioned that I wanted to keep going when the guy who spoke English interrupted.

"No, we have to wait."

"Wait for what?"

"Press is coming. They want to see you arriving. We have to wait for the press—radio and TV. Helicopter is coming. The whole country was looking for you . . ."

"Are you kidding me? You want me to wait here because the press asked you? No way! I want to go home NOW!"

I started walking again. I looked at the two men who found me and signalled for them to come along and show me the way. The others seemed to be trying to figure out what to do. They exchanged a few words and finally decided to come along too. We started down at a good clip.

The guy's phone started ringing again. He passed it to me as we kept walking.

"Hey JeanDavid, this is Stephan! We're so glad you were found! Oh, my friend, I hope you're OK!"

"Hi Stephan! Yes, I'm fine . . . I'm fine now. How's everybody?"

"Everybody is fine! We were all worried about you. We tried our best to find you!"

"Well, I found you guys!"

"Yes, I know! The village where you are, they just told me they heard you scream! Listen, Laurent wants to talk to you, hold on."

"Hey, JD! You really scared us, you know that?" From the sound of his voice, he meant it.

"Laurent! How are you? I'm so glad to be found. I'll tell you all about it. I haven't slept for three days! I haven't stopped partying, there were so many beautiful girls, it was crazy! You really missed out . . ."

"Quit it, you fool. Get back, you must be dying for a hot bath."

"No kidding, what with all my sweating."

"JeanDavid, this is Stephan again. A chopper is on the way. But you'll have to hurry up because he cannot fly during the night. And night is almost here. Can you give me the Nepali guy on the phone?"

I gave the phone back to its owner.

XXIII

"I Kill You When I See You"

My muscles were starting to hurt. After a few minutes I couldn't walk anymore. It was as though I had been struck down. My legs gave way, and I couldn't move. It was impossible to put one foot in front of the other. I held the arm of one of the farmers to keep from falling. Cramps wracked my legs, my back, and even my arms. I had been trudging for three days, straining my body at high altitude to climb, scale, jump, crawl and walk. At no point had I really suffered. Yet now, after all the sustained effort, my muscles were giving out. I couldn't move anymore. I was paralyzed. My body was finally calling it quits.

The helicopter arrived, but we were still close to a hundred metres away. The farmers held me up and helped me along. Each step was more painful than the last. The pilot ran over and tried to get us to speed up. In a few minutes he wouldn't be able to take off. We had to hurry.

The locals created a sort of receiving line, waving and clapping. I thanked them and realized that a lot of people knew about what had happened to me. The crew practically threw me into the helicopter, and we took off immediately. It was nearly nightfall.

When we arrived at the airport, a pack of journalists was waiting for us. Flashes, cameras, microphones everywhere. I was inundated with questions. One of the reporters was smoking, and I asked him for a cigarette. It was the first cigarette I had smoked in months, and I savoured it.

Laurent and Stephan ran to my side. Laurent instantly knew that I couldn't walk and didn't have the energy to face the journalists. He gave me a quick hug, took me by the arm and cleared a safe passage out of the mob. I found myself in a car. Laurent had been instructed to take me to the hospital immediately.

"No way, I want to take a hot bath. I want to go to the hotel. I have to take a bath, warm up, clean myself off. I'm covered in dirt."

"Of course, let's go. I'll call Stephan from the room. They can wait. Since you weren't there, they had to give your room to somebody else. So I packed your bag and put your things in my room. We'll sleep together tonight."

"Is it heated?"

Back at the hotel, I was so stricken that Laurent had to carry me up the stairs to the room.

In Pokhara, they cut the electricity around 7:00 p.m., but most places have their own generators. Laurent ran a bath, but the water was lukewarm. I couldn't stand being cold anymore; I needed to warm myself up and get clean. Luckily, Laurent found a teakettle and topped the bath off with boiling water.

I plugged in my phone to recharge the battery. I was concerned that Rebecca or my parents had started sending worried messages after having had no news from me in three days. When it was sufficiently charged, I turned it on.

I immediately received all the past days' texts.

EFI
THE ARMY FUND YOUR WING

The text was from 1:00 p.m. Saturday, barely two hours after I had left the ledge where I had spent my first night.

REBECCA
Hi Daddy!! What's up???

When do you get back, what time?
I miss you! Luv u

IRIS
Darling, how are you?! When do you
come home? Yvan and I send our love, Iris

At that very moment, the telephone rang.

"Dad, it's me!"

"My love . . ."

"Sorry, I know what you're going to say, I haven't called, I know, but I was with my friends. And then I tried to call you, but you didn't pick up . . . How are you?"

"My darling daughter . . . I missed you . . ."

"Me too! When do you get back? You must be having a blast flying with your friends. Be careful though . . ."

(A short silence.)

"Dad? Are you there? I can't hear you very well . . . Listen, I'm with Mom and we're about to eat. I can't talk too long."

(I got a grip on myself.)

"Yes, everything's great! Yeah, we've had a blast." I looked at Laurent, and he smiled back. "I'm coming home tomorrow. I'll see you Tuesday night, OK? Go on and eat. Say hi to Mom. But next time, don't forget, call me on the even days!"

"OK, Dad, I promise. See you on Tuesday then. Take care, I miss you!"

"I miss you too, baby . . . Rebecca?"

"Yes, Dad?"

". . . I love you."

"I love you too. See you Tuesday. Bye!"

I hung up.

At that instant I received a text from Efi.

> *EFI*
>
> *I KILL YOU WHEN I SEE YOU.*
> *DONT DO THIS AGAIN. LOVE*
> *YOU*

Epilogue

I had no idea what had happened during my absence. By the time I got to Pokhara, most of the other pilots from our expedition had gone home. Efi and Adam had taken a flight for Tel Aviv. François had left a note. The Belgians were also gone.

Laurent had stayed with the Russians to wait for me. I later learned what they had done for me, the energy with which they had organized the search effort. Some of them had gone to pray in the neighbouring temples. Word of their prayers had apparently reached the Dalai Lama, who, after meditating, had predicted I would return on Sunday.

Viktor had organized a tour of the area by PPG, taking off at daybreak with bags of supplies that the pilots could drop if they spotted me. They had taken serious risks, flying low in the mountains in cloudy weather.

Stephan and Laurent had also arranged for a search party with the Nepali army. More than two hundred soldiers had been sent into the mountains. They brought back my sail and motor, found just a few hours after I left the ledge.

The day after I was rescued, the town had a ceremony to celebrate my "rebirth." The soldiers who had searched for me and all of the local officials were there. They returned my sail and my motor and bestowed on me the honours of the town of Pokhara. I was very moved.

The entire town and a good part of the country had followed the news from the search parties—with the exception of the French Embassy, whose only concern had been whether I was insured or not. I later learned that if the French Embassy had made a single call to the Nepali minister in charge of the army, he would have immediately sent out two special helicopters with infrared cameras, based just half an hour away from Pokhara. They probably would have found me in an hour.

Thankfully, Laurent had rearranged my return trip with my travel insurer, who had very kindly reserved a seat for me in business class. That very evening, I was booked on a flight for Paris. Stretched out, wrapped up in a blanket, my head on a pillow—I was warm. It felt so good. The flight attendant offered me a glass of champagne, with a maternal smile.

But I barely noticed.

I was on a date.

For my parents;
for my daughter.

For Jimmy.
January 2012

Meanwhile . . .
Laurent's Story

Friday

I got news of your crash in the early afternoon. I spoke
with you on the radio. I remember telling you to avoid
sweating to keep from catching cold and to wrap yourself up in the sail to stay warm. We planned to come get
you the following morning.

Saturday

I spent a sleepless night. I imagined you alone, isolated.
Your radio cut out around 7:30 a.m. Between 7:00 and
10:00 a.m., Natasha, who had found your insurance
papers, asked me to call the French Embassy and tell
them what had happened. The embassy offered no help,
told me to call your insurer and refused to do anything
until they knew who would pay for the cost of your
search party.

Your insurer, Mondial Assistance, asked me for your
insurance number and copies of your pilot's license and
passport. They asked me to call back the Embassy so
that it would get in touch with the local authorities.

When I did so, the Embassy asked me to be the guarantor for your search costs, even though you were properly insured. The Embassy then sent me back to your insurer, who in turn accepted to cover only search costs up to a certain limit. I offered to serve as a guarantor for costs myself, but the Embassy just dismissed me.

I told Natasha and the paramotor organization that I would cover all of the costs if necessary and begged them to start the search. A representative from the Nepali army came to the organization headquarters and asked for a recent photograph and physical description. He wanted to know what kind of shape you were in, how you had been dressed the last time I saw you, whether you had any experience in the mountains and so on. He went back to his base and immediately organized the rescue mission. The previous night, they had already sent three trekkers to look for you, but they were at least two days' walk from your position.

Stephan and I left for the airport to take a helicopter. We were stuck on the ground for an hour and fifteen minutes due to the weather. We finally took off at 11:15. We went through the clouds at 11:30 and came to a position about eight hundred metres from your location. The helicopter landed on a plateau above that point. I walked for an hour and a half before nearly reaching your precise coordinates, but at about thirty metres away, the mountain became too steep—it was impossible to reach you.

We shouted and called your name, but we couldn't hear anything in return. The high altitude made it difficult to breathe. We looked for you until 12:30 p.m. Even climbing back to the helicopter was difficult because of the altitude. By that time I was really worried. I wondered how you had made it through the night up there, how you would survive if we didn't find you soon.

Back in the helicopter, we positioned ourselves on a direct vertical above your coordinates, but it was by then impossible to see anything—the clouds had thickened, and we had to turn back. We returned to the airport, and I went back to the hotel.

The organization told me that the army had launched a search party. They asked me to call your insurance company and ask for confirmation of your coverage by fax.

I thought the army would find you. Viktor and the Russian team weren't as confident and decided to take things into their own hands. They looked for high–mountain trekking guides in Pokhara; we bought supplies, things to drink and eat, bags, and we planned to search for you by paramotor.

Sunday
Around 6:30 a.m. the four Russians took off to search for signs of your crash site. They got up to about 2,500

metres but were blocked by the clouds and had to come back. I got angry with them because I was getting really worried, and I grew depressed waiting for news. We knew that the army had left with helicopters and trekkers. The Russians tried to cheer me up. One of the Russian couples went to the Buddhist temple to pray for you. They came back with marks on their foreheads.[3]

People from Pokhara started coming to the bar next to the flight club to comfort us. Many of them said they had prayed for you. A sort of group solidarity began to form as we waited together. The passing hours dragged by.

Around 4:30 p.m., I was in the bar talking to your insurance company when Natasha got a phone call saying that the villagers had found you. They gave me the number of the guy who was with you, and they passed you the phone when I called. I was so happy to finally be able to talk to you. You were near a village, about twenty-five kilometres from Pokhara. You said, "Laurent, I can't walk very well. I'm thirsty."

We were reunited on the tarmac at the airport. You were still wearing your motorcycle jumpsuit, walking like RoboCop. The hotel had emptied out your room, so I'd brought your things into mine. You wanted to take a bath more than anything, even though the organization wanted to you to go to the hospital first. When I was

---

3   These marks on the forehead (*Tiikaa*) are an auspicious sign or blessing.

moving your things, I found the jar of Nutella you always travel with. I made sure to set it out on your nightstand, but strangely, you weren't hungry. All you cared about was a hot bath. You had so much trouble walking, I had to hold you up to get you into the tub.

You gave me your GoPro and your camera and told me, "Copy all of the photos you want off of the GoPro, but not the video camera, it contains my will. Don't copy that."

When you took off your clothes, everything was wet and covered in thorns, dirt and mud. You couldn't get your socks off by yourself. I ran you a bath. You wanted to stay in the bathroom. Then I took you to the hospital. It was the worst place I've ever seen—there was blood on the walls. I told you, "Don't let them inject you with anything here, in twenty-four hours you'll be in France. Don't let them do anything here." But you seemed trusting. They took your blood. It was black. The wall next to your chair was streaked with blood. They took X-rays and put an IV in you for forty-five minutes. You hardly moved, you were so knocked out. I had to help you get dressed again and tie your shoes. You could barely sit up.

Afterwards, we went to a restaurant where a dinner had been organized. The Russians were overjoyed to see you. We all drank to your health, but you had trouble eating. Then we went back to the hotel, and you went to bed.

Monday

You decided to make donations to the town, to the soldiers who had searched for you and to the villagers who had found you. You went to every ATM in Pokhara to take out as much cash as possible. At the military base, there were interviews, honours, speeches, journalists. The army had retrieved your paramotor and sail and arranged them on a table like holy relics. You were honoured by the city of Pokhara and given a birth certificate. You made a lovely speech. Everybody was moved.

Finally, we left for the airport. We boarded for Kathmandu together. From there, I put you on your flight to Delhi, then to Paris.

While you were on your way to France, I was flying back to Canada.